lantana strangling ixora

poems

SASENARINE
PERSAUD

We acknowledge the support of the Canada Council for the Arts for our publishing program. We also acknowledge support from the Government of Ontario through the Ontario Arts Council.

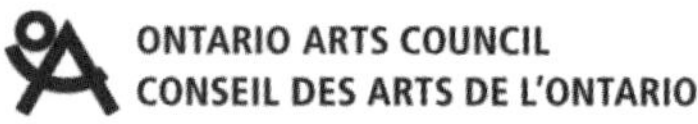

Cover Image: Peggy Stockdale
Cover Design: Peggy Stockdale

Library and Archives Canada Cataloguing in Publication

Persaud, Sasenarine, 1958-
Lantana strangling ixora / by Sasenarine Persaud.

Poems.
ISBN 978-1-894770-72-9

I. Title.

PS8581.E7495L35 2011 C811'.54 C2011-903255-4

Printed and bound in Canada by Coach House Printing

TSAR Publications
P. O. Box 6996, Station A
Toronto, Ontario M5W 1X7
Canada

www.tsarbooks.com

ACKNOWLEDGEMENTS

To Joe Nathan and *Confluence* in which the following poems appeared in slightly different form: "Americans Reinterpreting History", "The Pause", "Sketching a Windchime", "When", "Circumambulating the Parking Garage."

To *Muse India* in which the following poems appeared: "Festival of Light: Diwali"; "Bageshree, a Raga"; "Yoga Studio, Plymouth"; "Locating the Saraswattie"; "Marco Polo at Rama-Sethu"; and "A Coconut Branch Broom."

To Geoffrey Phillips for publishing "Walcott, Heaney, Muldoon & Co."

To TSAR, Nurjehan, and Moyez for following their dreams and taking me along.

The Lantana (also known as the purple lantana—because of the small purple/lavender flowers–trailing lantana, or creeping lantana, or weeping lantana), which forms the first part of the title of this book, is native to South America. It has been introduced and grown globally.

The Ixora (known by various names including: Flame of the Woods, and West Indian jasmine), which forms the other part of the name of this book, is a flower of Indian and tropical Asian origin. It too has been introduced and grown globally. Its flowers have long been used by Hindus in puja and worship. It is a popular flower in Guyana and Trinidad (countries where people of Indian ancestry form the largest ethnic groups), and in South and Central Florida.

CONTENTS

LANTANA STRANGLING IXORA

There were times in the morning
we questioned the bloom
of the previous evening, watering
canna lilies, clearing the live oaks'
acorns from our white wrought iron bench.

How do ripe plantains smell?
Like ripe bananas. You could laugh
until after dinner. I will hold
Radhakrishnan's interpretation of the Upanishads
until you switch on the ceiling fan

And we twirl on the sheets of a different seeking
scented like lilacs in a north-of-Toronto park
or the Arnold Arboretum. If you recall
a dead British poet with the same last name
would you be wrong? American literature

or flowers in Florida gardens
are all we need to know except
if "Papa" is traveling in the hills of Africa
or Buck is observing Chinese. You drift
into a naked sleep where snores sing

and a mouth that has taught us Kali's secrets
falls open to accommodate blocked passages
or water the definition of a flower cluster
or the naming of a southern plant—datura
as prickly as a morning when the alarm

failed and you're late for a meeting

and we barely have time to glance
at the golden marigolds: left foot right foot
brake and accelerate through amber lights
impatient with ancient drivers mesmerized

by dew on the St Augustine grass and the pointed
ficus leaves a replica of Rama's arrow-tips—
We barely have time to see lantana strangling ixora.

HOLE IN YOUR HEAD

These were sixties-seventies pictures.
But nobody warned: look out
for calf-boots and mini-skirts. Look out

For that sucksand between black
leather and blue denim hem,
a black car's back seats costumed

With audition accessories, Hollywood-
beckoning to eyes overlooking the Charles.
An autumn wind sprinkling hair sprigs

Between lips as you comment—
There is no need to raise a hand,
wait a turn. We are, if not friends,

Familiar. Do we need to see your tongue
sucking on a pen's head, almond
eyes, senorita, sparkling like a gypsy's

That Indian-summer day in fall
you selected tan open-toe shoes.
Thin straps circling ankles

Like peacock feathers in our eyes
mesmerized—Bostonian is a shoe type,
a magazine with maple-red covers

A girl drawing arrows in the hearts'

margins, a woman parting
her hair in the middle

Like a Hindu bride awaiting
that red sindhur's rubbing
from forehead to hole in your head

QUATTRO

Mirror no larger than a laptop's screen
or a British Guiana postage stamp
stuck on a hallway bedroom wall

—catching more natural light—
The only mirror in the house
except mommy's rotating vanity

In a bedroom we hardly visited
since she departed. Eyeing your morning
ritual in front of the stamp-on-the-wall,

A whisper mustache straight as a ruler.
The froth-milk lather brushed on, swiped
off in sequence like the old scythe-man

Along the Queen's College cricket
field edges. Tongue puffing cheek
on one side, tongue puffing cheek

On the other—elastic skin—
the British blade reaching growth
below expanded surface

For a cleaner look. At least, until tomorrow
you are unscrewing the handle from
the safety razor cap curving the frail blade

And rinsing in a dish. A postage-stamp-sized

metal wafer cleaning rubble from your face
and you set out for work on your Raleigh

Until, unexplained, you stopped. It returns—
in a florescent dawn facing a wall-wide glass
hoisting this gift: a razor with four blades.

HALLOWEEN

He who never talked much
to neighbours and locked his garage
even before he left or entered

Was the first one out at dusk—
garage door up, lights flaring
like nostrils or a movie dragon

Dr No. Why do you sit in a lawn
chair with candies in a sack
for the ghostly procession. Children's

Parents looking over shoulders
scrutinizing every expression. We'll
let you know we are here if needed.

We turn around on another year.
Your ghost spiriting up the stairs.
I unaware, shirtless, unprepared.

You are too early or else too late
to knock or read my door-taped
notice: do not come with an actor's

Makeup kit on your face.
Do not conceal cheekbone, forehead,
nose, or chin, peeking through

Orifices shaded by your education:

to continue attraction to love
only if attractor and attractee

Are single. Or searching last year's
bookshelves for the spirits crafted
by someone else. If you come

to my threshold, if you press the lit
buzzer or music your knuckles
please come with eyes, soul's portals, undisguised.

YOGA STUDIO, PLYMOUTH

When we stopped,
it was as though two uncles spun castnets
in the swirling evening light

On serpents: red criss-crossed
with tire-dark stripes and a mist
thick as a turkey's winter-feathered breasts

Stretching out across the Atlantic
east and south. A propagandist
writing an essay on "Early English Separatists"

We celebrate at Thanksgiving, skipping
the first two years they stole from each other
to survive, or the natives' hospitality

And hostility—you S our land
you S our birds: in another century S=sample
not—"Look!" You exclaim, in a Columbus voice

As the lights flicker on. "A yoga studio!"
We twine lips around fingers around limbs between
clipped hair and the long ride back to a Boston night.

A SERPENT ON THE FLATWOODS TRAIL

Stuck and staring from the blacktop
snaking through green slash pine and scrub palm
still glowing from long departed summer rains.

Staring at wheels flashing in the tea-weak sun
at expensive soles pounding the tarred trail
like infantry in a keep-fit-stay-well army.

Frozen in the warm December wilderness
one said, "The cottonmouth was frightened.
We've invaded its space." A rollerbladed pair

Glides into the rest-water-information station
shorts displaying shaved calves and muscled thighs
tanned a Florida golden cream rising: down stroke

Up stroke, down stroke, up—Biblical proportions—
Mythologies you may not care to believe,
or peddle like Jehovah's Witnesses, do not make them untrue.

WALCOTT, HEANEY, MULDOON & CO

But for those unfamed
not this trudge and toil
of backside on swivel chair

Eyes glued to monitors and digital
counter adding minutes and hours.
Eight Internet Explorer windows

Open to funds moving between
Europe, Asia, the Middle East, and
the Americas: Where are the money

Launderers? You can track money's
pathways and cannot find your own.
You can justify an electronic transfer's

Journey and forget your name's
origin until a remittance's laneway
lands you an alert in MP, UP, or AP.

Where is that? Uttar or Andhra Pradesh
are states in India—a Cebanova's in Romania
Lorca's nostrils flared by a Roma

Andalusia performance perched
in a Boston library in oil mostly black
the cloth of flamenco dancer's skirts

And singers' shirts enough to encircle

sun like a yolk rising over water
invisible from the highway's tar-top snake

Lined with pepper-red eyes on SUVs'
behinds; those unfamed lower down
on a Ford road—another day chasing

Electronic-money-millionaire-companies
Arab entities or Chinese investing in the chair
you sit, the backlit screens you examine

For rent, or an hour to compose yourself.
Would we not prefer "fame" and Sunday's
emptiness, the whoredom of a poet: words

You do not write a poem, the anointed and their acolyte
critics say: you *attempt* to write . . . they have, of course,
you eat put-you-down pie and serf for a Saudi Prince

For those without Arkansas or other testaments,
for the visionaries who said, once, the chosen
dwell in a certain region, and only gods could fly.

RAKING THE LAWN IN DECEMBER

Waiting for the wafer-thin winter
sun buffered by a dawn fog
lingering past midmorning

Like an illicit lover's scent—to see
what lies beyond the summer
lawn. The heavy rake's a pelican

Sifting this green-blond inlet.
How many weekly mowings' half
mulched accumulation—contrary

To manufacturer's specifications: it'll
cut and mulch or rear bag, your choice,
two in one. For a healthier look,

Let the clippings return to soil
and wetlands apportioned
and deeded. Gently gather snips

Built up from spring through fall—
Steel fingers on a stray pebble
chiming is a neighbour's

Cartwheeled by a careless edger.
She was trimming along your
common line near the magnolia

she always wanted in her yard—

You'd understand if you were born
In the Deep South. Is it a year since

She gravitated to a larger lot. Perfecting
a yogi's asan, whispering a mantra: "Do not,
do not disturb the unseeded grass' secrets."

MORNING E-MAIL

Is the song's Swiss chocolate percolating
all we wait for in the dawn
there are few sounds—the refrigerator's
humming is a retreating surf,
a coy mistress adrift in a skiff,
currents planting across the Gulf
of Mexico or California's cold mountains.
But it is warm inside. The laptop's weaving
for a Windows application. Outlook Express
connecting. Not even the mockingbirds
warble. Later, in the mid-afternoon
glare, if not covered by the brushfire's
haze, the two years' drought-induced restrictions
are enforced by the water police. Or is the song
a white Swiss candy? We've been addicted to
Cocoa's descent down South American slopes.
What we shared in words, in digital media,
millions have, too—no consolation, yet, you
message: *it was a special thing, time, was it not . . .*

LOCATING THE SARASWATTIE

Wading through financial reports
in the Philippines you heard yet again
"India has no sense of history."

An Executive Director's car, a house
on the hill, bonuses, a salary as sweet
as kheer—hearing again that parroted tale:
India's epics are fables. Replaying
an old newsreel, "Thriller in Manila"—placing
it all in an envelope and walking away
to validate that past: Vedas or Upanishads
or Ramayana or Mahabharata, you knew
the Rishis were ace reporters of their times;
your explorers wading through scientific
swamps, tracing shifting watercourses,
satellite photographs, village mounds,
sedimentary highroads and stranded towns.

It was not enough that NASA's images
and Indian Navy divers located Dwarka,
Krishna's city in the sea. It was not enough
that skeptics halved their laughter.
Myths, they chuckled. Myths
until you found *her* flowing like winded hair
dancing under the Rajasthan sands,
changing course over the centuries.

Not a thousand years' invasions
through mountain passes or desert seas.

Not the Turking of the Tejo Mahalya—"Taj!"
Not the frocking unfrocking missionaries.
Not the manifestos of failed communists
discredited in Moscow or Havana thrown aside—
so many sand grains flying in the wind.

Rolling back the muslin of unbelievers' mockery,
is there any question? India's epic Quartet
is a history of a world, her River still feeding
a vermilion land: the Saraswattie no longer
legend. Sacred Saraswattie not fib: fact, fact, fact.

DADDY, AFTER DINNER

Speckled with its own design
like lime skin pickled in vinegar,
the arborite kitchen countertop

is spotless. You've washed the dishes
wiped the aluminum drainboard
scrubbed the blackpot from the cast-iron

karahi—Today, the force-ripe wind
whistling through the front windows
taunted the buzzing kerosene

two-burner stove; the downturned
kero bottle gulping; air bubbles rising
like balloons manned by novices

when the wind throws a tantrum
the flames pulling down—no son,
it's not sediments in the kero.

The curry simmers. The warm roti
is wrapped in a cotton flourbag
towel, the loose Red Rose tea leaves

steeping in a five-pound tin saucepan
teapot. If your mother were here—
Daddy, you would have done the same . .

We are having dinner in the fertile

new-cleared old plot of silence;
you, on the back landing overlooking

the alley, the laden jamoon, the giraffe
plum tree grazing coconut branches
frequented by tanager, bunting, kiskadee

six o'clock bees, really beetles,
transporting souls into a wounded sky
still celebrating evening-time.

You might well have said, *listen.*
You might well have said, *take*
my musician's soul to songs

you need to record in studios far away.
It is no different today as we dine
overlooking the backyard and balding

cypresses swinging their Spanish-moss
beards; one more swipe with the rag
and the chrome faucet sparkles.

Dishes air dry on the rack.
The tiled tabletop looks
like a dentist's advertisement

for rejuvenated teeth. The formica's
clean-speckled like a snow tiger
and you're still sitting on that landing

and you are still listening and saying:
one day you should record this concentrate
of pitris dancing in the after-supper dusk.

GLOBAL WARMING

A wren screams in the startled night
or is it a blue jay stalked by a cat.
Winter bird, winter bird you have dallied

too long. Ice in Nunavut mistakes
March for a July thaw. We will not
see you here next winter will spring

in Georgia or South Carolina. Beachfront
properties will sink into seas. The neurologist
smirks and mutters: nothing new

under this sun, I've read the Mahabharata
as a communist reading a tract on faith
depends on evidence makes science

fact: Krishna described the sinking
of Dwarka into the ocean—golden city
located by satellites and Indian Navy divers.

See, it's all cycles. You cannot stem
the tide. The Dutch are bolder: break dykes
let the water come in where it may.

Let no dove scream in a flooding night.
He who values beachfront mansions
will be worth more when water touches his door.

CEREAL

Tiger now native to the USA
smiling on the shelf
you rewind to Esso's animal

winking and hauled to court.
You can no longer
put that cat in your car.

It will cost oil-producers
and futures-traders
a monopoly clawed

by wind farms and solar panels
spotting rooftops, corn harvests
leaping to ethanol and gains

long eluding farmers.
We are feeding vehicles
in the breakfast aisle

still too many choices
the same peacock dazzling
boxes: honey bunches of oats.

THE NEW FORMALISTS

Our time will turn on a chakra
again, my love, if heart dominates
art's hot air pumped into vermilion

pepper and Dublin green balloons
floating into morning skies must come
down in an urban field contemplating

a museum's blooded heels and campus
minds. I bring you no Heaney
Walcott successor—professor at Oxford

or Princeton falling back on Elizabethan
metrics—was that a puffed up wig
she sported concealing a bald head;

a wired skirt hiding Sam's Caribbean "pussy"
is an embarrassment to some West Indians
walking on the commons by an embankment.

In the end, Raleigh was caged in the Tower.
First poetry on Guiana, London's stagecraft
creeping up on his head for his heart

hanging on South American trees—a fable
from ancient India travelling to Europe
and beyond learned syllables ploughed

for linen phrases and multiple meanings.

A yogi must cleanse his soul in the bush
you'll find no designer shrubs or driveways

—any path, every path your own
Brahma Vishnu Mahesha—I know none
no artifice in this jungle of your love, love.

ADJUSTING TO PROGRESSIVES

After the affair, televisions replaying
that finger spearing air you, too, spotted
the half-empty glass: political spouse

wronged, re-calibrating the road back.
Last week, at the eye glass fitting,
the assistant advised: progressives

are a tricky thing. It is how you look—
follow your nose. Whirling her head
and hair like a cast net and tossing

a Southern smile, as if to demonstrate.
The grace to forgive comes from a mind
on the campaign ahead not the Gulf, the Gulf, the Gulf.

BEACHCOMBERS

An upturned sole cemented
in sand from the tide-dump
on shorelines of past embraces.
We are tracing footprints
along the water's edge
tiny impressions, deep indented
heels, pointed toes, out steps curled
like the neck of an orgasmed crane.
And you may be correct.
Her imprints are more eye-catching
but in the coming tide tonight
all is erased on linen clouds—
saffron limbs on a just-laundered bedspread
saffron specks in the nude's painted eyes
glowing in the dark like rubies.

IN SPRING

Forsythia flaring up
in a yellow match-flame
in the drizzle's progression

to showers and an overcast
hurrying you to the parked car
on the honey locust hill

still budding Hollywood vistas:
On the Charles River rowers
and mountain ranges in a frame

snapped from an antiquated
digital camera, a smudge
of dark shoe polish in an eye

and your quip from Los Angeles—
Do not dream of fall
when you are in spring.

SKETCHING A WINDCHIME

Blue plumbago waving frantically
in high wind the brass chimes
echoing an emperor's garden
after he has withdrawn his hands
from a courtesan's shaved legs
the kingdom's burdens and labours
are shifted in the official painter's
brushes water pink and lime bamboo
cured to engineered floors fitting
without nails or paste
interlocking Channels clicking flush
like bodies in a spoon and birds
coming out as tentative as deer
the wind subsiding and retreating
leaving you clutching a pen
manufactured in Guangdong Province

MARCO POLO AT RAMA-SETHU

Silken threads known
before his journey
to the Emperor's court

recording on that passage
Rama's bridge across the ocean
from Tamil Nadu to Lanka

Raghu's vanaar army—how inebriated
can you be if monkeys talk
in an underwater crocodile wife's

yearning for monkey-liver-soup
to cure an ailment: man shooting
too much breeze with another

must be curbed—building a stone
causeway to confront Ravana—
You do not negotiate with terrorists.

THE PAUSE

Pausing in the heat to pour water
around new planted shrubs:
Formosa azaleas still turgid
from last night's watering.
We misplaced the wheel's rhythm.
It was not possible.
We could resume at will.
Periwinkles snuggle up to marigolds
over ripe carrots bloom
because we failed to harvest them
last fall. Lantanas wait on winter.
You whispered goodbye and turned
your face to a land and time we loved
and could only recall in a mirror of tears.

LONGFELLOW BRIDGE, BOSTON

Curve of eye and breast
the instep of feet examined
from down under discarded

beach attire, the architect's
vision twinkled that premature dusk
through the wall of snow on the river.

THRUSHES

Call and response, once
singing notes so similar
it was whispered we echoed

Each. Who was the parrot?
Wind rushed in from another
direction bouncing off bone-grey

Staves splitting along dog-eared
edges ribbed by portholes
of fallen wood knots.

Delay and divergence crept
in and you could hear
without listening: call. No response.

MONGOOSE MEN

(a spat between VS Naipaul and Derek Walcott)

The windows are double-paned
hurricane strong. We throw
no stones from this archipelago's

slingshot traversing the Atlantic:
O lord, mongoose in an English
henhouse! Rodent scurrying

to an afternoon sale of vaginas
sex slave—do not mock my Cuffy's
fingering Dutch plantation mistresses—

would he not know condensed milk
limbs like Norwegian spruces swallowed
by a Boston snow blowing—a new master

strutting down Commonwealth Avenue
an almond-eyed playwright weeping,
twice injured, a long way from Jerusalem

or Brooklyn mistaken for Brookline
or the flaming Poincianas of Coral Gables
substituted for Georgetown samans

mongoose man let us not pelt missives
at our rodent cages waiting for the next experiment
on paper—we are all mongoose men.

MONGOOSE ON SNAKE: Nightfall on Walcock

The chickens squawked intermittently
that night. Fowl thieves stalking nightmares
and an empty pen in the morning

we saw him perched on a coconut branch
daddy chuckling and pronouncing its name.
Not rat with a long tail dangling

like a truncated Tarzan vine. The chickens safe
from their feathers shed in fear. Fewer serpents
scurried about the grass we weeded with patwas

and twenty-twos for the annual sowing of bora
seeds and purple-hued baigan and emerald-
leafed poi-bhaji. We shed a fear of vermin

in the laden palm with the pink clara nuts'
flesh glowing like the women's leg lips
we would come to know later—cane-sweet

juice leaking down the sides of our mouths
full of cream-soft jelly. The creature had served
us too with a pride of origin—*afraid*

to say Hindu, she mocked, *and you reading*
DA Walcock! Swirling her dreadlocks
and white cotton skirt like a gypsy dancer:
Never trust a West Indian man talking about nightfall!

RIVERS AND HISTORIES—KENNEDYS IN IMAX

Whitewater rafting from Massachusetts
where the Atlantic pounds the coastline
and green waves run the Vineyard bays
like wind over savannah grass, first father
and son set out to sail a thousand miles.

We bring daughters, now, take photographs
for posterity: a senator; snaps taken
after the Civil War. The first man to sail
the Colorado's length was a one-armed
veteran honoured with a lake called Powell.
What happened to his team? They mutinied.
Some died. And yet in a Boston fall
where ivy rusts on a concrete wall
Harris recasts a surly crew
negotiating rapids in a Guiana bush.

Take One: a shot rang out and Donne
is dead. In another, they sail into the interior
guided by an old Amerindian woman
and the enchantress, Mariella. Surveyors
mapped the water; the natives leading
from the rims of cliffs are forgotten
until you reconstruct *a Palace of the Peacock*
in London or—on a New England river bank
scullers don red and white and work
like Canada Geese in precision flight.

You cannot drink this water from the Charles

a British king's nomenclature bonded
to a revolution's waste runoff—
all rivers are one river, all waters one.
Fifty years to wait for a swim
in the Charles or Colorado. Father guiding
daughter in an IMAX domed theatre

The green-logoed university
across the street deserted on July 4th.
Did you pay for the second feature?
asks an attendant. We produce the passes
stashed in a teenage purse. Receding lights
bring up the Gobi Desert and dinosaur

fossils in New Mexico Badlands. The rain
is gone in the morning after the fireworks—
chewing carrot cake laced with coconut
shreds and sliced pineapples. The gazebo's rust
belly is proof the Chinese manufacturer
has lied. The steel deteriorating faster
than water tumbling over rapids. Powell,
now, was one-armed. How could he take
a boat through those torrents alone;
how could he be the first man to sail
that thinning ribbon river?—we know,
Robert, your narrative was scripted
elsewhere. History is made by the media,
truth by dreamers, madmen, poets . . .

BEACH HOLIDAY

As we were pulling out
she leaned over.
It seemed by accident.

Spouse melted into a mirage
on the Gulf sand with a child
must go. We do not know.

Engaged in strapping the cycles'
steel limbs to the bike rack—
at highway speeds you do not need

debris or liability—the van's door
pulled back: hungry boys
are biting into sandwiches

in the shadows of Australian pines
we negotiate sponge-brown needles
clustered on the trail, minced shells

and tethered dogs. How many things
can you gather in a crowded park
or a training course's first session?

And yet, as we were pulling out,
she leaned over to fix something
on the floor near the front seat.

Digital pictures fade when reproduced

on paper in verse—no panties beneath
swim shorts displaying Dutch edams

removed from wax-red wrappers
and your ties to nights in cities
you cannot name in that pause

pulling out, checking behind
for other drivers glancing in the rearview
straightening cabbage-cut hair

in the window-glass reflection
a needle hole you've entered before
turning back to that long journey home.

GUERILLAS

Raiding imaginations and Greek epics
Biblical stories or Rama's, a genealogy
stringing a thousand-verse caravan,

mammoth webs were concocted, epics and
classics from the wider Caribbean. At 30,000 feet—
litres and metres yet to harmonize sky travel—

the water in this south is like a navy uniform
or the rinse your mother made dissolving
a "cake of blue" for making white fabric whiter.

Straddling a continent's coast, the Atlantic—
if you have your way would become
the Adriatic or Caribbean Sea—soon giving way,

before coffee's quite finished, to the Trinidad
outline—"Why is it called a small island?" asks
the dreadlocked teen, peeping over a shoulder

she had dozed on earlier in the dawn.
It can fit a dozen times over in Guyana.
It nurtured little men nibbling Homer's fictions

or Ram Lilas staged on Caroni's dusty plains.
On the island's tip, oil platforms flare in water
and burn off unwanted fuel; bank right

bank left. "Ladies and gentlemen, we are making

our descent towards Port-of-Spain." Mist
like thinning silver hair attempts to camouflage

the headscape of the land. Searching,
you find no bald spots, no brown scrubland
no runway burning fires, no flames, no dust

except for postage-stamp buildings, everything's
a Kaieteur-gorge-green. You cut off a piece,
a straggler tail-tip in a serpent archipelago

of islands connecting to the Florida peninsula,
for a keepsake—a teardrop—not for epics
or lies or fictions or literary reportage—

"Mr L is writing a tome on . . . Guyana"—but because
you are all guerillas, ambushing yourselves
and all imaginations for your next whatever book.

NO POLITICS OF THE PAST

Revisiting Georgetown after twenty years

Having reclothed themselves,
supporters of the deceased
dictator say, your love poems

sing. To tell the truth there was
a Catholic girlfriend's eyes
igniting the Brickdam Cathedral's

shaded entrance and Dutch-planted
silk cottons from other centuries
conducted by the North-East Trades

a symphony stringing limbs
and later in the curtained room:
I always thought you were Hindu.

I am. And you will not convert?
Shaking your head sideways
the muted sobs in the white pillow

case mingling with a whine
of changing gears outside—
dependable British automobiles,

difficult to tell apart
the cotton and her face except
the eyes like the blue flames

of a gas cooker just before
the valve is shut off—
you take separate paths outside.

What if. What if we said, "Yes"?
Old scars remain on our limbs.
After twenty-five years, the photos

reappear. Rehabilitation of a tyrant;
supporters chanting love! Love! Love is all!—
do not dwell on the politics of our past.

PLEA

After twenty years—more—
flying past on a motorcycle,
Atlantic wind still whips

a wisp of hair on your forehead
a sacred dot—to circumambulate
the Sanskritic fire crackling

under the tent; a twisting garage
stands guard now a doghouse.
I forgot my vows; exiting

the Canadian embassy with a visa.
Clasp me from behind, once more,
from the pillion rider's seat

from above a snaking consulate
line, from a land beyond
this ocean's roaring; broken promises.

Could you ever encircle me again
On this Raleigh-failing coast
Straddling a Japanese engine or forgive

me forgive me forgive me for forgetting.

REPLY TO, "A WHITE MAN CONSIDERS THE SITUATION"

"Black sentries are whispering"
Says one who is privileged
By position, by a Cambridge degree

And a cotton skin. I speak as one
West Indian by breeding—
Without ancestral tree as one

Who mended his own trousers
With multi-hued scraps before carnival
Was foisted on this land as one

Who walked barefoot through puddles
And on the burning grass
Parapet because the tar puddled

Like quicksilver in an August sun as one
Watching you in a British car
Chauffeured by a uniformed Indian

Zipping by to meetings with the "comrades"
And the "Great Leaders" who ran
This land into numbered Swiss accounts

And rigged ballots. Today we shake
Hands and exchange pleasantries and listen
To another fib, you say, "I can never

Leave this country." At least not in the months

Of Canadian cold, snowbird to South America
Today we shake hands as one

Poet clothed in the epics of Europe
To another freighted
In the Upanishads—truth is not the same

In all cultures. Skin is not the same
In all cultures or love for those who can afford
"black sentries"—and those who cannot.

A COCONUT BRANCH BROOM

In a corner unused
a collection
of palm frond arteries
stripped and bound
at the top
a tropical broom
they send as gift

to brush congealed flour
fallen off a kneading bowl
off thawa saada roti
swelling like a craupaud
how do three boys prepare
dinner—who will cut
vegetables compose dough
wield belna sakay roti
stir the pot and afterwards
who will wash the dishes
sweep the kitchen floor
on schooldays on holidays

a matter for he
with that ancestral gift
for gab or he
who talks the most
in public he with a Sanskritic
penchant for details he
with the most published
memories repeated often
fiction assumes fact

FICTION AS SHRINK

Striding down Park Avenue
or Yonge Street like the last Bourbon
as the Towers crumple in dust

returning to an apartment
missing half occupant
a partner down in smoke

grief flying south of the border
then heading north to Boston
you tell an ancient man

you cannot have so many women—
in fiction women gravitate
to your heroes like nails

to magnets like you're
Mr IT—and the loss of a fiancé
is more than the loss

of a mother at eight
and in fiction that justifies
murder in a Manhattan bathtub

FESTIVAL OF LIGHTS: DIWALI

Lifting Shiva's bow
from a cradle of dust
string humming before
a crack of unused wood
limbs igniting
the archer's fingers
words kindling palm fronds
dispelling a thousand years
repose Lakshmi to Vishnu
Raghuvamsa Raghuvamsa
Raghuvamsa

SIR VSN SENDS GREETINGS TO WALCOTT ON HALLOWEEN

Do not stand before my door
With a mask on your face

Leave this to the literati
To she who would labour fiction

Leave this to the world-worn
In a boat buffeted by winds

In a small regional sea, a charcoal
Man straddling the boat's bow

In a white singlet, a torn trousers:
Batman, Wonder Woman

Spidey, odyssey and Trojan
Imitation imitation imitation

But do not stand before my door
Do not knuckle my portal

Or stab my buzzer with macaw
Colours on your face

I will come to you unmasked I will
Adorn the rivulets-lets sweeping

Your mouth and your forehead
With Upanishadic seeking and ashram laughter

But do not pose before my threshold
With a borrowed fable on your face.

PHOTO GALLERY: BERENICE'S MELANCHOLY

Wind bent branches
like rabbit ears
against a pig-iron sky
melting could be dawn.
It is dusk, I tell you
während wir sprechen
während wir sprechen
German if I know a language
by script. How does a picture look?
A thousand Myspaces
clamouring for attention.
We are reading ourselves
posting thumbnails
by thousands. Click on a word
hatching links like ants.
I can love you
if you tell me how. Pose
by a camera steadied
on a tripod; post another
a mother walking in a park
a lit bridge in a night
substitute for stars
a companion's frozen smile
I could love you
if you tell me how. Click
on a mouse. What did Ganesha
mean? I will love you
if you tell me how.

THREE WISE MEN, CHRISTMAS 2008

They squandered no time arriving
in corporate jets. You have no plan
the whipped Republicans wailed
like pampered schoolboys—the Democrats;
come back. Drive. How did those elected
representatives get to DC? Who came by
surface from Florida, from California?

The three wise men from Detroit
returned in hybrids and left empty-hearted
without fanfare. Wise men know
when not to speak or ask
a Congressional Inquisition or reporters
flashing cameras like macaw feathers—
how many of you drive Japanese or Korean
or German automobiles wounding
your economies. Wise men come
in the night on horse, or camel, or ass.
It must be these that gestured: silence is golden.

A HAMMOCK IN THE WIND

Balgobin Bidatha Singh, Sept 1913–Dec 2008

Your axe as clean as a new razor
cleaved logs to firewood like knife
on thawed cheese, down stroke the arc
of a butterfly. You taught us how to walk
lightly on the earth—leave no footprints
behind; how to peel an orange,
the honed twenty-two a penknife in your hand
producing an unbroken string of rind dangling
in the wind while negotiating a footpath "aback."

Resizing a fallen tree trunk, chips flew
like starbursts. Rock gently in the bottomhouse
hammock and hum Tulsidas' poem for the ages:
Shri Guru Charan Saroj Raj, Nij Man Mukur Sudhari
Barran Raghuvar Bimal Jasu, Jo Dayaka Phal Chari . . .
With the dust of guru's lotus feet, I first clean
The mirror of my heart, then tell the story
Of Shri Rama, giver of the four fruits of life . . .

At ninety-four you are sipping tea
and laughing at sugar—*I consume two pounds*
every two weeks!—needing no cane to walk
or no aid to memory: the grip of a teenager.
How to compare palms and trace strength,
the thorns of a tangerine tree, unshouldering
a bunch of fresh-cut plantains, how to tie
a cotton band around your stomach—a brace
for back—before sinking the fork into the soil . . .

Who scattered those ashes in the ocean,
and sprinkled a handful "aback" on this mother
earth you taught us to love, humming
the *Hanuman Chalisa* in the wind of your wake
the vacated hammock swaying like a kite-tail.

IN JANUARY

Even in January when the cypress
Has gone bald, there is clutter
From the past: Spanish moss, you say,
Confederate gray like the beards
Of Hindu sages stroked by the fingers
Of wind. A meditation or a yagna,
Chants from a thousand yogis—
You are who you are; who are you
You are who you are; who are you

A man whose mother was white
Is African-American. Even if you play
On words like that other "lawyer"
In the *White* House (I did not have sex
With that woman) an African father
Makes you African—if you are
Born in good ole USA! Who knew
You were another lefty?

Reporters take a raccoon's ass break
On race except you mention noose
Or words beginning with "G" or "F"
Or "N"—Namaste Namaste Namaste
Chant the yogis in unison
You are who you are; who are you
You are who you are; who are you

CIRCUMAMBULATING THE PARKING GARAGE

Once you're in lefty
it is right and right and right
and you can stalk cars
forever—Olds gone, GM going
Chrysler's way. The history of automobiles.

Ford's blue egg hatching
another fusion. The freight train's horn
awakening a new year's slumber
dissolved in the Carolina wrens' chirps.

Once you're in lefty
it is left and left and left
until your tenancy's over. Who slept
in what room, how you redecorate
bush immaterial except to the woman

whose ancestors served in factories
plucked cotton on plantations
bore the brunt of a one-eyed recording—
you are viewed by your car:
a lowly Ford, Bavarian Motor Works
or Japanese Kaizen sipping gasoline

so the myth goes once you're in you're in
and it is left and left and left
and when you're exiting right
into those very books you once condemned.

STEPPING BACK

Stepping back from this island
you would call a continent
by definition, the middle-schooler
laughing; all continents are islands—

Stepping back for a telephoto view
of coconut trees spiking every skyline
in a dusk settling like fine
ginger grounds swirling the world

in a gallon rum-jug: a local brew
distraught by a blaring disco
a flashing television's lightening,
cars cawing the evening

ensconced in a library growing
from suitcases of mutual acquaintances
returned; gutters falling off roofs
concrete houses hotter than Everglades

summers—we do not know Hades
like that Homer of the Islands
making Grecian imagination carnival
in Port-of-Spain—where are the white-eyed

parrots and the fowl-cocks, laden red pepper
beds, double marigolds necking Canna,
dray carts clip-clopping. Sobbing at the end
of the other line, you will not see me again . . .

And you cannot explain: we could never
come back to that we left behind—the envy
of a less complicated time, our world
just two points, then: India and British Guiana.

NAIPAUL INVENTING "HAT"

In a Georgetown zoo
that was how the monkeys sat:
knees up to chin knocked
ankles apart saki-winki posture
like that one inhabiting
a great-grandmother's yard
or an aunt whose husband
traipsed deep in the bush
eradicating yellow fever
in a staged picture cowboy hat
on a horse strumming a guitar
a mountain behind an Amerindian hut
mountain behind tarmac to the plane

you never said, "Great One," what type
of plane, mountain you lifted like
Hanuman bringing the leaf-of-life
to those colonies we peopled—
even England was falling apart,
Nothing a way of seeing the world
from the backroom of a converted hotel
'rangutan my father would toss
from tongue, langur view upside down
picking fleas off a typewriter's keys.

IN THE PARK, TOMORROW

Wind scratching leaves like shells
the seashore in the rising tide's refrain
a song we know—you cannot stop
this train to Washington tomorrow
a prophet takes office—I have a dream

—this recession will recede. You step
past green palmettos, a herd of sheep-
jawed deer sailing over the black trail
flicking white-tipped tails and waiting
for a timid young to cross further down

an eastern bluebird sheltering in a shrub
from the gust of arctic air. Tomorrow's
inauguration heralds a King Midas.
Further, the palms throw dead branches
to the frost-burnt grass, not caution.

Tomorrow the streets will be paved
with gold; the ash-grey deadfall heap
trapped when last summer's floods dried
will disappear on the taking of an oath.
At the trailhead, as you pull out, another
pulls in—another search. There was no
El Dorado, not even in Raleigh's head.

BAGESHREE, A RAGA

Washing crumbs from dishes
and following your dance
across a continent

soles slapping wood elevation
fingers fruiting the air
no hit and run or hit

and miss; poet loves
India from afar in kathak
or bharatanatyam or Moguls

decapitating pakawaj and palms
offstage slapping stretched goat
skins—was I dear friend an album's

chant: Allah Allah a faint chorus—
I didn't know you in that Toronto
Fall face to face or through this "net"

a raga we couldn't find
didn't need a name to exist, or
a false title—"Emperor"—to thrive

AFTER THE HARD FREEZE

Ganesha, you know, I've never flown
to Asia. Lazuli earrings dangling
on hips. Blue jeans that have worn

better times. Death of a sibling
in childhood, or a mother, stays with you.
Were it not for the photograph

I could not remember she who clutched
me in her womb. There is that mirror
in your eyes—passion for the living

emanating from that cut down in prime.
This frost in February was the worst.
Everything went straw-brown, a flaxen

touch in your hair flung over a shoulder
extolling the neck of a gazelle
or a white-tailed deer sailing over a trail

you cannot touch. The chainsaw lives
on the neem's unmarked limbs
cluttered with freeze-burnt leaves;

the "shami" next—Indian orchid reduced
to a stump. The pen-and-ink's black
glowing beneath a morning clothed

like a cotton-covered futon. We sit

on edge perusing highlighted passages
glowing like yolk-mixed paints

on an embossed Bible manuscript. Stepping
out, slippers exposing unvarnished toes—
men don't wear nail polish! Ha! Ha!

Next, pruning the palms—fuzz curling
like private hair, the phone ringing far away
over the din; a message: you're wanted elsewhere.

COUCH

You've forgotten
what it's all about.
You've made your peace
with the chair.
The garbage truck brakes.
The bins clutter to the driveway.
There is no room to throw limbs
like those lines your uncle tossed
into that confluence
where river met ocean,
settling down for a nibble;
finally, you've earned
his fisherman's face and, no doubt,
your long wait on the couch.

LETTER FROM THE PAST

Spanish moss tumbling
from trunk to unclipped lawn
must go for a memory:
a tossed towel
ending a night's erratic breathing
or exclamations
to Biblical personages

We work better in the dark
we work better unspeaking
on the uncut grass
the moss tumbling off leave-taking
limbs on a book that inks your name

TO KEEP US

In the Bahia struggling
through the winter blahs
pin-prick flowers bloom
a Florida spring in February.
Iris-sized nuggets
in the frost-thrashed grass
are the lawnkeeper's nemesis—
the dreaded clover blossoms—
midwinter we welcome
petals from that wildflower patch
now understanding your saying:
a love to keep us in old age.

MAILSTOP

Nothing in the post
since our cyber age—
no blade-edged envelope
no scents enclosed
by saliva or tonguelick
no serrated thumbprint
offering a window on the world
and now nothing
in the inbox
but a passion dissipated
the shouts of Internet entries
silenced in unyielding boxes
like yogis eating cakes
created from space.

WHEN

And when that time arrives
—as it must—when we part
may there be no taste of neem
on our tongues—what might have been
is in dreams and our next mornings
the smooth transitioning motorcycles'
gears trolling our dull neighbourhoods.

THE CELL TOWER AT PRIDE ELEMENTARY

It might have been after she fell
And hit her head. But she returned
In time for the show and the farmer
Spouse who came with a towering
Knife: why wait for one-a-day?
The School Board's not wood—sawdust
Glued together—Gut schools.
Web the sky. Deceive flags and crosses.
Imitate pines. Radiate palms and pupils
Who dare to look or question the folly
Of slaying the goose for investors' eggs
Scrambled—like children's minds—
In RF Radiation, in principals' fibs
In a Board's uncaring. Intransigence,
You say. It was after she hit her head.

THIS OTHER PREGNANCY

Turning away to other cares
and things and now turning
back years we had not seen
your sharkskin shorts
—was that all you ever wore—
contoured and rippled legs
reddened toes kissing concrete
outside the porch door—do you
have sugar? I ran out
a tumult of indigo stars igniting
eyes we knew what the Amazon
looked like until this moment
womb laden like an orange tree
in season head down into text
messaging like a shamed cat.

VOWS

Who placed that dot
On your forehead
We ask forever—Krishna
Might have been
An answer were you Mira
It is not this person
I've become he
Who cannot recollect
Promises cannot honour them

AMONG WOMEN CRITICS, WOMEN WRITERS

Flaxen hair cascading
Like a waterfall around a smile
Editing typos concealing

A loss on September 11
Makes a hero in Manhattan
Or a Columbia degree

An authority on fictions:
How to murder
An unfaithful male lover

Or toss a neem comment
On male fiction
Where women flock to a raja-like

Protagonist plucking women
Like feathers from a fowl
In boiling water—ridiculous!

You say. Your companions agreeing
Awaiting the break to enthuse
On the next episode or movie

Of "Sex and the City" in NY women
Exercising their libido—a new
Boy-man victim five nights a week.

THE NUTS

Of an evening when the soy stick
Tastes rubbery and the mockingbirds
Sound off key and rebellious.
When night doesn't lower her skirt
Gracefully, when beetles bang
On your ears like boys
On black-potted saucepans on a South
American summer's day when adults
Are away. When cold coffee tastes
No worse than rank well water
From a country tap, you can laugh
With the Brooklyn boys' colloquialism
"The nuts are still shooting a mean flame!"

PLANTATION BACKDAMS

Following Uncle Georgie
deeper into the canals
of Ogle Estate, swimming
to another sideline dam
sugarcane stalks swishing
in an afternoon breeze
skimming the Atlantic

and the deep trenches
from his childhood—
a Doberman's tail—rich
with fish, "Look out for hassar
bursting." Even as we shouted
"there" Georgie spinning
the castnet like a flamenco
dancer's skirt: a glimpse
of a life we'd never know

the peacock hued sunfish
dancing in a lead-heavy net
before he threw it back
before we recrossed the swift
canals empty-handed picking
guava and baby jamoon
on the way out of that old
plantation to another

ELEPHANTS IN THE ROOM

When did the Great Wall slip
into our dining room? Perhaps during an Italian's
journey to the Emperor's court thirsting

the art of papermaking, or noodles, a British eye
for fine teacups and dinnerware
cheap in WalMart, or not, in Staples.

Forget the Long March, the concocted hunger
in the Cultural Revolution. It is too late.
Tanks snake on caked red and separated flesh

in Tiananmen Square the cleaners scrubbed
all night: the new proletariat cheering their first
astronaut in space. No elections in 100 years

or was that 1000? From panty to scissors
clipping your private hair made in C—thanks.
The boys in Havana brandish hand-me-downs

Stalin-era Kalashnikovs and tanks running
on water. An arrow in his throat or thigh
Ponce lay dying in Havana like the cigar rogue

can't lift a wiry beard. Was a time when
a descent from the mountains,
when mention of that name sparked

a fireworks of laughter or departures

and the exiles the exiles the exiles, and I
who should be one, holding DC on a leash.

Washington and the soldiers who crossed
the frozen Delaware moaning in graves.
But turning his tail to the tiger, swatting a flea

with a long trunk, taking off for Trinidad;
in his quest for El Dorado, Raleigh landed near
Piarco according to fables penned in the tower

before the executioners, blind men from states
in the Americas line up in Port-of-Spain
for the show—to feel the trunk of an elephant

Sir Walter's untouchable not like Clinton in Miami
—I'm smarter—an Americas Summit with Cuba
in absentia! I bring you change—all that's left

from the billions to the Wall Street millionaires.
A left finger shaking: We are not Islam's enemy,
we are Havana's. We are not China's enemy, we are Cuba's.

FINDING AMY C*

We may have crossed
eyes, or followed the sway
of your sex in a street lined
with ginkgos. Holidaying in NYC
who cannot afford to be generous
to one who implores the visitation
of words. Images abound in this city's
City—a starling-street-gang displacing
a wren, glass walls rising and multiplying
summer light: take another swig
of toes in pumps at rush hour heading
home—this swarm's no movie's—
to fruited houses or apartments
animated by TV or a waiting cat.
You might get lucky. Not here

One thousand miles south
in a book sale languishing
among poetry titles. I know nothing
except the blurb and took you
anyway—so many words and yet
no say. The ash tree cut. Your leaves
dispersed to my fingers; breath in ears
your bounty sailing on this page.

*Amy Clampitt (1920–1994)